Dreamer's Handbook

Written by Lisa Regan

Miles Kelly
PUBLISHING

Contents

Dream catching

How many times have you woken up with a totally real picture in your head – and then realized it was actually just a dream? Sometimes your dreams might wake you up in the middle of the night, and even make you wonder where you are. Other times your alarm clock will burst in on a great dream and you'll wish you could snooze a while longer to see what happens at the end of your adventure.

Have you ever tried to figure out what was going on in those dreams? It's tricky, because most dreams disappear before you've even got to school to be able to tell your friends about them.

For as long as people have been dreaming, there have been other people who were interested in dreams. Many people think there are parallels to your waking time, and that you dream about your brother because he's a big part in your life. Tying his shoelaces could be a symbol that you feel you're always having to look after him. Others think it's even more simple than that, and you dream about the bus and an octopus because they rhyme, and something you saw or talked about made you think of one of them before you went to sleep.

More recently, scientists have tried to study dreams and sleep patterns. Psychoanalysts from the end of the 19th century, such as Freud and Jung, had theories about what dreams might mean (read more about this on pages 10–11). Psychologists have studied brain waves during sleep and found that activity in our brains increases and affects whether we dream or not.

How to use your handbook

Think about it. Even if you could watch a DVD of your dream, would it make any more sense second time around, when you're awake? That's where this book comes in. There could be hidden meanings in your dreams – you just need to be able to read the signs. First, you have to learn to make your own equivalent of a DVD, and train yourself to remember and write down everything you can from your dream. Then you have to study what the dream is all about. Your dreams can be happy, sad, scary or downright weird, but there are sure to be some lessons you can learn from them if you know how to read the signs. Your subconscious mind could be trying to tell you something – so it's time to learn to listen. And the best thing of all? You can do it in your sleep!

What's in a dream?

The obvious question to ask at first is, "What exactly IS a dream?" It can be defined as a story you have in your sleep – although the chances are it won't be like any story you've read or seen on TV.

Dream stories often involve a mix of real and unreal people and events. You might recognize someone you once knew, and your mum, and some people who don't have names or faces but play a part in the story. The story might be set in lots of places, zooming from your playground to your grandma's kitchen and then off again to a street you don't recognize at all.

Dreams often seem kind of crazy because of all the unrecognizable elements, and it's very common for them to change location without any reason or sense. Scientists who study dreams think that we try to make sense of random events because that's how we deal with waking life. However, it might be the case that dreams don't follow a logical order like that.

Studying sleep

Modern technology has made it possible for scientists to study our brains, even if we're sleeping. Electrical scans and brain imaging (like MRI* scans) can show what our brains are doing, and this can be linked to different emotions. So a scientist can tell if your dream is making you happy, scared or sad.

However, science isn't quite clever enough (just yet) to tell us what you're actually dreaming about to make you feel happy – your dream could be about your favourite person, or a great exam result, or receiving a wonderful present.

What science has learnt so far, though, is when most dreams occur – usually during the last couple of hours of your sleep, just before you wake up**. That has allowed dream analysts to teach people the best ways to remember their dreams – and that's what you're going to attempt while you read this book!

*MRI scans are Magnetic Resonance Imaging – a person can be moved through a machine that takes a picture of the inside of their head or body to see what's going on underneath the skin.
** Read more about sleep patterns on page 74–75.

Dream meanings

So, we know that remembering our dreams is like watching a weird and wonderful movie starring a few people you know in real life. But what does it all mean? That's a question that started to interest scientists around the start of the last century. Before that, though, dreams were equally important in different ways.

Australian Aboriginal tribes tell their history, and stories of their present and future, through 'dreamtime'. Native American tribes believed that dreams were vitally important and could be used to decide what action to take. You may have seen their dreamcatchers – carefully woven strings in a circle, decorated with feathers and shells. These are said to allow good dreams to flow through the holes, but catch the bad dreams like a spider's web.

In many western countries, dreams were used to pass on religious messages. In the Middle Ages, dreams were said to be the work of the Devil, tempting people while they slept. Many religious characters were visited in their dreams to pass on divine messages to the rest of their believers.

In some tribes in Australia, even today, they believe that snoring allows your spirit to leave your body for its own adventures.

Science and Psychology

Nowadays, many western people take a 'psychological' approach to dreaming. They think that dreams help to show us what's going on in our unconscious mind. If you secretly want something to happen, or are worried about something but don't think about it when you're awake, elements of it will creep into your mind and show themselves through your dreams.

Once scientists had figured this out, they started to look deeper into what dreams can tell us about ourselves. The earliest people to do this came up with some theories that people don't even believe any more. However, they did pave the way for people to start analysing dreams in different ways. The next pages deal with the main psychoanalysts and what they thought dreams were revealing – or hiding! – while we slept.

Field Of dreams

Sigmund Freud (1856–1939)

Freud was really the first person to study the role of dreams in our unconscious mind. His book, *The Interpretation of Dreams*, was published in 1900 and started up much discussion about the subject. He thought that dreams were the part of us that we don't want to reveal – unconscious thoughts that we hide from our conscious self. He developed 'free association' – a way of talking about the dreams, which eventually led to the issue at the root of the dream.

Carl Jung (1875–1960)

Like Freud, Jung believed that people have an unconscious self as well as a conscious one. However, he disagreed that dreams were hiding unwanted thoughts. He thought that dreams were our way of telling ourselves what our fears and desires actually are. Jung also believed in a 'collective unconscious' – a group of symbols found in myths and stories that were relevant to all humans, all around the world. He thought these symbols were important in dreams.

Alfred Adler   (1870–1937)

Adler thought that there was a direct connection between dreaming and waking life. Our dreams could show us how to solve our problems. He said that the less you dream, the fewer problems you have. He thought that dream symbols were simple and direct – for example, if you dreamt of flying, it showed ambition, or nakedness showed you were scared of being made to look silly in public.

Medard Boss   (1908–1990)

Boss took the simplest approach. For him, dreams had a single level of meaning, and reflected what is happening in your waking life. His belief was that all humans create their own reality and have the power to make their own choices, and that dreams just help us to make those choices.

Frederic (Fritz) Perls   (1893–1970)

For Perls, the human mind is very organized, and tries to fill in any gaps to make sense of things. He felt that dreams were 'emotional holes' that your mind is trying to fill in. He also thought that many parts of your dream were aspects of yourself – so your mum actually symbolises your own wish to mother people, and a chair is your own reluctance to get off your bottom and act on something.

Dream Dictionary

Following the work of the people you've read about, many other people started to investigate what dreams might mean. Some dream analysts think that objects and people in your dreams are symbols of things in real life. Breaking down your dream and looking at the meaning of separate parts can give you hints about what to do when you're awake. Other dream analysts don't believe it's so simple, but it's a great way to start taking proper notice of your dream stories.

Admirer

If you are being admired, **it's a good sign for the future.** You should keep your friends, and they will respect you, even if you rise above them in life. If you are doing the admiring don't panic! Consider what it is about them that impresses you. Perhaps you simply wish you were a bit more like them.

Anchor

This could show that **something is holding you back** – although it could be your mind's way of saying that you have to struggle through your problems to find solutions. It's generally a sign of hope and success.

Angels

A great sign! **People's respect for you will increase**, and so will your good reputation. Just be careful they're not in your dream to tell you off for something bad you're feeling guilty about in actual life.

Do you dream about relationships?

See Argument and Kiss

Apples

Look forward to a **long and happy life!** If you're eating apples, and they taste bitter, you have to be prepared for some misfortune or hard work along the way, but with the same happy outcome.

Argument

Not surprisingly, this dream could be because you're **unsettled** in waking life. Are you in the middle of a fall-out with someone you're close to?

Do you dream about travel?

See Bicycle, Flying and Journey

Army

An unhappy dream showing worry and fears. Are you troubled about wars in the real world? However, if you join the army in your dream, it shows **you're feeling strong** – nothing can harm you. If the army is on the march, it's a good, successful omen.

Baby

Although babies are cute, and this dream ultimately means **success and happiness**, look closer. Dreaming of a tiny baby indicates that you're too dependent on others.

Bald

This could show that you're worried about something (even if it's not about losing your hair!) – try to get to the root of the problem. It's often **a sign of loss in your life**.

Balloon

The sight of a floating balloon is linked to a feeling of frustration or **unreached goals**. You may have to struggle or even change tactics before you see results. If you're in a hot air balloon, it's time to lighten up and look on the bright side.

Do you dream about landscapes?

See Mountains

Banquet

Unfortunately, this is a **sign of hard times**. It might be that you're worried about money matters, or that you're feeling hard-done-by emotionally. You need to be 'fattened up' with love and attention.

Bat

A bat flying at night is a sign of money worries or family rows. Make your own mind up what to do, because others may have a **hidden agenda** when they offer you advice.

Bath

You need to 'wash away' things you're hanging on to. Forgive and forget as you might be clinging on to troubles. If the water is dark and dirty, there's more undoubt ahead, but if the water is clear, **things will be better** from now on.

Bed

Dreaming you're in your own bed is a good sign that you're settled and secure, and have **good self-knowledge**. If you're making a bed, you could be moving soon. Someone else's bed is a sign of decisions you've taken – how you feel about the dream is a sign of how you feel about choices you just made.

Bees

A sign that you'll **profit from hard work**.
A bee sting isn't so good – you may have a small
argument with someone you care about, or have your
reputation damaged by careless talk.

Bicycle

This dream suggests that you're in the middle of
making a decision. If you feel safe on the
bicycle, you should trust your instincts. Sometimes
the dream shows that you're trying to balance different
aspects of your life – maybe your friends and a new
boyfriend, or your social life and school work.

Blood

Don't be scared if you dream about blood. It's not a
bad sign of things to come! If you're bleeding, then it's
a sign that **you're overdoing it**. Slow down
before you wear yourself out. If it's an animal bleeding,
it could be telling you that you need someone else to
share your responsibilities.

Cage

A birdcage is a symbol of happiness in the future, especially in your love life. If the door is open though, beware of being deceived by someone you fancy. If you're the one in the cage, you're **feeling powerless** over an area of your life.

Do you dream about education?

See Exams, School and University

Candle

If the candle is lit, **a pleasant surprise** is heading your way. If you light the candle, it's a sign of trust and faithfulness, perhaps from your loved ones. Often, burning candles represent your own quest for knowledge.

Cards

If you're winning at a game of cards it's a good sign, and suggests that you will be successful in waking life too. However, if you're losing the game it can also suggest a **run of bad luck**, so watch out – especially if you loose because you've been cheating.

Castle

Castles are often a sign of **conflict or arguments** with others. However, if you live in the castle, it could be that you're going to get rewards in life for your honourable behaviour.

Do you dream about the body? See Bald, Blood, and Eyes

Cat

If you're a cat lover in waking life, these animals show luck and happiness in your dreams. If not, unfortunately, they're a bad sign. They could mean you're asking for others to betray you. If you chase the cat away, you'll **turn the tables** though and turn bad luck into good.

Cemetery

Don't panic! This is actually a good dream. Cemeteries are **symbols of hope** for the future, and the ability to overcome problems in your life. If the cemetery is in a bad state, the problems may be big ones, so you'll have to work hard to get past them.

Crying

Dreams where you're crying might seem distressing, but they usually mean that some sort of healing is happening in your life. You're successfully **overcoming obstacles** and moving on.

Death

This is **NOT a bad omen** – no dream can predict that someone's going to die. If you know the person, it could mean that you wish you could be more like them. Dreams about dying do sometimes suggest that you're feeling worried and pessimistic, though, so try to find out what's causing the worry.

Dolphins

Dolphins are intelligent creatures, and so represent the state of your mental health. If the dolphin is leaping and soaring then things are **great for you** right now. If you're swimming with the dolphin then you're feeling very optimistic.

Drowning

A drowning dream suggests you're **feeling overwhelmed**. If you survive the drowning in your dream, it shows you're strong enough to get through the hard times. If you drown, or are saved by someone, you need to ask for help in your waking life, as you can't do everything on your own.

Ducks

These birds are a great sign – they bring improvements in your waking life, possibly linked to money. If the ducks are swimming, you have the **strength to survive** people bad-mouthing you, as you're popular enough to get over it.

Eagle

Dreams of this bird are usually linked to your ambitions and expectations of yourself. The eagle represents strength and pride. Dreaming about a soaring eagle is a great **prediction of your success**. Baby eagles in a nest represent your social status rising.

Do you dream about water?

See Crying, Ocean and River

Earthquake

This dream suggests that you're feeling **stressed or nervous** about something. It could be that you're fearful of changes that are happening to you. If the earthquake lasts for a long time, it's likely that you're worried about someone close to you.

Do you dream about captivity?
See Cage, Prison, Tower, Wall and Zoo

Exam

If you're actually revising or sitting exams, then this dream is just your mind working overtime. If that's not the case, exam dreams usually suggest you're having difficulties in some aspect of life. Dreaming about revising, though, is **a good sign** – you're a hard-working person who's reliable and a good friend.

Eyes

If it's your own eyes in your dream, it's a message about you as a person. If the eyes are blind, you need to **face up to things** rather than ignoring them – or 'turning a blind eye', as the saying goes.

Falling

This is a common event in dreams. If you fall and aren't hurt by it, it shows that you will **overcome problems** you're faced with in waking life. If the fall frightens you, it's a sign that something is troubling you. You might be struggling with a problem and need to look for help.

Fish

Swimming fish are the symbol of your own **inner self** – so in a dream they reflect how you're feeling about your own insights. For example, if you catch one, it shows that you're focusing on what you're thinking. Cooking and eating fish are more linked to your energy levels and brainpower.

Flowers

Generally, flowers are a sign of **happiness and good luck**. Colourful flowers suggest that someone has been very kind to you, but white flowers are a sign of sadness in your life. If the flowers are dried up you may have recently had a big disappointment in your life.

Flying

Mostly, flying dreams are good dreams. They show a **feeling of freedom**, with you in control. Flying over a huge crater or abyss means you're being annoying and insufferable. Flying in a chair or bed suggests that you want to travel.

Do you dream about spirituality?
See Angels and Ghosts

Forest

Wandering through a forest spells trouble – you could be **taking unnecessary risks**. If you actually get lost in the forest, though, you're on the verge of success.

Garden see also Vegetables

If your dream garden is full of flowers and wildlife, then you're a romantic who's looking for love in your life. You're a caring type of person who likes to look after people. An overgrown garden indicates that you're **neglecting your inner self**, or your spiritual side. Look inside and be nicer to yourself.

Ghosts

Ghosts often represent an aspect of your own self that's bothering you. They could be a way of **recognizing fears** that you're burying. Take a long look at yourself when you're awake, and see if you can figure out what you're denying. Sometimes they're a symbol of something that you need to let go of.

Giant

If you appear in your own dream as a giant, you're struggling with an **inferiority complex**. If you're battling with a giant, you've got problems in life that you're dealing with. Try to figure out what your battle is, and look for ways around the problem.

Gold see also Jewellery

Dreams about gold jewellery or bars show that you need to be more careful with money. Finances are causing you concern. If the gold is made into plates you're happier with the situation and may be getting more money. Finding gold is a sign you have **great abilities** and will storm ahead of your rivals.

Gun

If you're loading or firing a gun, take note! It's your subconscious telling you to stay calm and not lose your temper. If someone else has the gun, it **indicates an injustice** – this may be to you, or to someone close to you. Hunting with a gun is a sign that you're putting off making a major decision.

Hammer

This usually means that you're **feeling discouraged** about something you want to do. However, if you're hitting a nail into wood with it, you're feeling more successful.

Do you dream about holidays?
See Island and Paradise

Hatred

This isn't good – you're **burying bad feelings** that are coming through in your dreams. It may also mean that you're feeling victimized, or are forcing your own opinions onto other people. Investigate now to stop these dreams!

Head(ache)

Dreams with heads in signify your view of the world. If it's your head, and there's no body, or someone is trying to hurt your head, then you're not **looking clearly** at a problem. If you have a headache in your dream, chances are that you're going in the wrong direction because you're not thinking straight.

Heat

If you think you felt hot in your dream, you're **embarrassed or ashamed** about something. If you're warming yourself in front of a fire, your imagination is heading out of control.

Do you dream about food?

See Apples, Banquet, Fruit and Vegetables

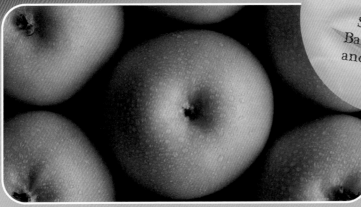

Horse

There are several aspects to horse dreams – think of the different sayings about horses. Have you been 'horsing around', or do you need to 'get off your high horse'? If these don't apply, the horse symbolizes physical energy – do you need to **harness that energy** in a positive way?

Insects

These are symbols of obstacles in your life. If you swat at them and they don't go away, you must concentrate your waking thoughts on solving the problems. If they buzz off and leave you alone, **your mind is settled** because obstacles have already been overcome.

Island

A fairly common theme in dreams. Being stranded on a desert island suggests that you're **bored with your life** as it is at the moment. Many island dreams are ones of contentment, though. If your island is a nice place to live, then you're happy with life at the moment.

Jewellery see also Gold and Necklace

This is a symbol of things that are precious to you, especially personal qualities. If the jewellery is stolen or lost, you're feeling inadequate in waking life, and want to improve yourself. If you're given jewels then you're **headed for happier times**, and will be more content with the way you're living your life.

Journey

This is a dream about 'finding yourself'. It's very much influenced by the scenery on the journey – if you are walking across an open, bare landscape you feel there's **something lacking** in your life. If there's someone travelling with you, you may find in waking life that you're scared to attempt things on your own.

Jungle

This signifies a **tangled mess** in waking life – it could be your lovelife, your finances or your friends that are in a muddle. If you're following a path through the jungle it means you're about to resolve the mess, and clear up any of the issues that have been holding you back.

Kiss

Kissing in dreams is usually good – it shows you're **feeling happy** in a relationship. Don't worry if it's someone you don't fancy – it could just be that they've got qualities you admire.

Do you dream about emotions? See Hatred and Loneliness

Knife

This is a warning dream. Your subconscious is trying to tell you to **be careful about something** you're going to do. Being cut by a knife is a warning that others are bad-mouthing you. If you're the one holding the knife, you have something that you need to cut out of your life as it's having a harmful effect.

Ladder

A straightforward sign – climbing up indicates success, falling down suggests that you'll struggle in something you're **trying to achieve**. If someone is holding the ladder for you, you'll get where you want to go if you accept the help of others.

Leaves

Green, healthy leaves show that you're happy with the way things are working for you right now. Fallen or dead leaves suggest **you're having difficulties**, or aren't feeling great physically. You may have lost hope, and feel sad or in despair. Ask for help!

Letters

Writing a letter is great. **You're happy emotionally** – maybe you're even in love? Getting a letter means you're waiting for news, but be prepared for it to be bad news. If you dream what the letter is about, it's a definite message from your subconscious – it's just finding new ways to communicate to you.

Light

Great news! You're on the verge of 'seeing the light' –
finding the answer to a problem, or learning the truth
about something. Moving towards the light suggests
that you're looking for **more stimulation** in
your life, probably intellectually.

Limp

This suggests a **lack of balance** in your
relationships – are you taking more than you give,
or the other way round?

Do you
dream about
animals?
See Sheep, Snake
and Tiger

Loneliness

This dream may sadden you, but don't be scared. It usually means that you're such a **sorted person** you can guarantee you'll always have people who care about you. It can sometimes mean that you're feeling rejected or misunderstood.

Mirror

This dream can indicate vanity – if you know that's one of your faults, sort it out now! If not, then it's usually a sign that **you're scared** of trying something – so take a look at yourself, and have more faith in your own abilities.

Do you dream about birds?

See Ducks and Eagles

Money

Money can represent your own self-belief and feeling of self-worth. If you dream of finding or winning money, it shows that you can **be successful** when you try things. Giving money away suggests that you're looking for love. If someone else is giving it away, you're probably feeling neglected or ignored.

Moon

The Moon is **a symbol of change**, but also of recurring cycles. Your subconscious could be warning you about something that's become a habit. If it's a full moon, something has just reached completion. A new moon, then, suggests that you're about to start a new project.

Mountains

Climbing a mountain signifies ambition and achievements. If you're on top, then **you're feeling successful**. If you're struggling up the mountainside, you're facing obstacles that you must overcome. If you fall from the mountain you're in too much of a hurry to achieve things.

Music

You're **feeling relaxed and happy**, and your sleeping mind is enjoying itself! That is, unless the music is too loud, or out of tune – that's a sign of mental distress and disturbance.

Do you dream about careers?

See Army and Police

Naked

If you're naked in your dream, it's a sign that you're fearful of exposure. It could be that you're **hiding a guilty secret**, or that you're scared of being shown up and made fun of in public. If other people are naked, and you feel shocked, it suggests that you're afraid of finding out the truth about them.

Necklace *see also* Jewellery

Seeing a necklace worn by someone else is a sign of your own jealousy. Look inside yourself to see if **you feel resentful** about that person. If you're wearing the necklace, it suggests you're not altogether happy with your life, and have unfulfilled wishes.

Needle

If you find a needle in your dream, it could be that you're **worrying too much** about tiny things. Using a needle shows that you're hardworking, although it could show frustration over tasks if you dream about threading the needle. It also suggests that there's something you want to fix.

Ocean

Sailing on a calm ocean is great – things are going well for you right now. Troubled waters, as you'd guess, means that you're **mulling over problems**. If you're standing on the shore looking out to the ocean, your future actions might save you from a nasty accident – be on your guard!

Old

Old age suggests that you are leading a **peaceful and honest life**. Dreaming about old furniture, or buildings, isn't so good – there's something in your life that you should get rid of.

Do you dream about space?
See Moon and Stars

Oven

Is the oven hot or cold? Hot is great – good fortune is on its way, thanks to your **unselfish actions**. Cold isn't so good – you're causing arguments or heading for a bust-up. If you're cooking just for yourself in the dream you need to be more generous, and consider other people's needs as well as your own.

Palace

A dream involving a palace is a good omen for the future. You are **striving for success** and feel that it's almost within reach. If the palace is being built, expect a change of plan.

Paradise

A tropical paradise suggests that money is important to you, so you will try to earn enough to be secure financially. Many paradise dreams suggest that you're trying to **find spiritual perfection**, maybe to the extent that you're not living in the real world.

Piano

This musical instrument is a **symbol of harmony**. If you're playing it, you're searching for that harmony in your life. If you can hear piano music, it suggests you've found harmony already. Lucky you! If the piano is out of tune, you need to pay attention to an aspect of your life.

Pillow

Dreaming of a clean, crisp pillow shows that you're happy with life as it is. It's a great **omen of success** and happiness for the future. If you can't lift your head from the pillow, you may be needing some mental stimulation or support. It could also be that you need to rest more.

Police

A dream involving the police suggests that you've got a **guilty conscience** about something. Look inside yourself to see if that's the case, deep down. If you're the police officer, maybe you've been meddling in someone else's business a little too much?

Prison see also Cage

If you're the one in prison, this strongly suggests that you're being stifled, and **can't express yourself** as you'd like to. If someone else is in prison, it could mean that you'd like them to be taken out of your life. It could also mean that they represent a part of your personality that is being held back.

Purse

Do you dream about losing your purse? That suggests you've lost touch with the real you, or are feeling that **you're losing control** over an aspect of your life. If you've got your purse safely, you're keeping something about yourself hidden from other people.

Do you dream about the weather?

See Thunder and Rainbow

Queen

Dreaming about a queen is often a sign that you've got ideas above your station. Make sure you **listen to other people**. However, it can also mean that things are going to go well for you – have confidence in your abilities and things will work out right.

Rabbit

These fluffy creatures have long been a symbol of good luck, so if they appear in your dream you're **feeling lucky**. They may signify that you've been thinking about children, too – have you got a new baby in your family, or a pregnant relative?

Do you dream about wealth?
See Gold, Money, Purse and Riches

Rainbow

Great news, especially if you've just fallen in love. A rainbow shows that you've found someone who suits your personality, so you have a good bond together. If you're single, a rainbow is the sign of **hope and success**. It's a symbol of the link between your normal, earthly self and your higher, more spiritual self.

Riches

If you dream that you're really rich, it's actually a sign that you're **worried about lack of money**. If you're poor, the opposite is true – money has stopped being a worry for you.

River

Slow-flowing rivers are good in dreams – they're a sign that you've had good fortune, even if you haven't recognized it yet. If the river is fast, dangerous or muddy, then you're more worried about being in a **tricky situation**. Falling in shows that you're worried by a dangerous situation.

Roads

If you're walking along a road in your dream, then be proud of yourself. You're going to be rewarded for being a worthy person with good intentions. A wide road shows that your **relationships are in good health**, but a narrow road suggests that someone you've just met is bothering you.

Running

Running is purely a sign that you're avoiding an issue in waking life. If you're running away from danger, it shows that you're just **not facing up to your own fears**. If you're trying to run, but can't move, it's a sign that you're lacking in confidence and belief in yourself.

School

You should take note of how you felt in your dream about school. Was your dream school **a safe place** or an unhappy one? If the school wasn't your own, it could be your subconscious telling you that you're learning lessons in life.

Screaming

This dream strongly suggests that you're keeping your **feelings bottled up** inside. They're probably not good feelings, either – are you angry or scared? If you scream but no sound comes out, you've got to face your fears right now and get things sorted.

Sheep

Here, your subconscious is telling you to try new things, and to **be braver**. You can do things on your own if you just have a little more confidence.

Do you dream about bugs?

See Insects and Spiders

Snake

Generally, a snake is pointing you to someone in your life who can't be trusted. They're often a person who's your love rival, or someone trying to destroy your happiness. Occasionally, a snake is a symbol of your **knowledge and wisdom**, and is involved in showing you about positive changes to be made.

Spider

These creatures suggest that you're on the edge or outside of something. You may be **feeling left out** in a group. If there's a spider's web in your dream, then you're working really hard and should be rewarded for your efforts.

Star

Symbols of fame and fortune, stars show either your **faith in your own abilities**, or your ambitions to rise above the rest.

Do you dream about love?
See Admirer and Kiss

Thunder and Lightning

A violent storm is an indication of thoughtlessness – is it you that's been guilty of that? You have an important **life lesson to learn**. If the lightning is the main element, then take heart – good luck will help you.

Tiger

Tigers represent power, so your dream concerns your ability to **cope with power** – maybe your own, or maybe your attitude towards it. A sleeping tiger is safe, so a good sign, and could mean you'll go far in life. If it's attacking, it shows you that you're scared and can't handle a situation.

Tower

Bizarrely, a tower could signify a reversal in your fortunes. So climbing up in your dream might be a warning of a fall from grace. A tall tower suggests you could be caught in a **sticky situation**. Starting to climb the tower could be the beginning of a journey where you find out more about yourself.

Trees

Leafy, green trees (perhaps with lots of fruit) are a sign of future luck and blessings. Climbing the tree gets you closer to **ultimate happiness**. Leafless or uprooted trees suggest fear and annoyance. Don't waste your energy on useless things, or you'll suffer for it – possibly by losing a good friendship.

University

Shows ambition and open-mindedness. If you're applying to get in, **you're a strong-willed person**. Actually being there suggests you're having mood swings between happy and sad, unless a lecturer or professor is the main part of the dream, which shows overall happiness.

Vegetables see also Garden

You should **consider your health**. Seriously, it might be your body's attempt to tell you to eat better! The vegetable featured in the dream can be what's significant. For instance, orange carrots are a symbol of optimism, and green beans a symbol of wealth and prosperity.

Walking

How easy is it to walk? That's a sign of how many problems you feel you're wading through in waking life. Take note of where you're walking to, as this is significant. If it's grass, it's **a sign of calm**, but sand or snow shows that you may feel insecure. Walking at night is a sign of sadness.

Walls

Dreams about walls are easy to translate: they **signify obstacles**, so if you climb over them, that's a great sign. If you keep looking for a way around, you should reconsider how you find solutions to problems in waking life.

Do you dream about pets?

See Cat, Dog, Horse and Rabbit

Washing see also Bath

If you're washing an item such as clothes or a car, it's a great sign of **health and happiness**.

Do you dream about nature?

See Flower, Forest, Garden, Leaves and Tree

Weeds

Dreaming about weeds symbolizes a need to symplify your life. If the weeds are in an overgrown garden it may mean that you have neglected a certain area of your life. If you were removing weeds from the earth then it means you are **taking control of your life** after a busy spell.

Yawn

Take a **look at your life** – it seems you're not stimulated enough by what you're doing. It could be that you need emotional or intellectual change. Perhaps your brain is trying to tell you to get out and about more, to experience new, exciting challenges.

Zebra

A zebra usually appears in a dream as a warning. Look at **what you're aiming for** in a project, or in life, and check it's really what you want before you carry on throwing all your energy into it.

Zoo see also Cage

This could show that **your life is chaotic**. Take control, but make sure you're not feeling caged in. Each animal can symoblize a particular area of your life, so carefully consider what animals seemed the least content, and then think about what part of your life that animal might relate to.

How to record your dreams

To be able to look at your dreams properly, you need to keep a Dream Diary. You must have noticed before now that the most vivid dreams soon fade into nothingness when you get up and start your day. Before this can happen, you should write down your dream details.

Keep this book by your bedside so you can write in it as soon as you wake up. If you've just had a dream, write down everything you can remember – the following pages give you lots of room to start your own Dream Diary. If you're not sure where to start, ask yourself the W-questions:

Who is in your dream? Are you the main character? Who else is there?

What is the theme? What emotions (eg happy, sad) and sensations (eg hot, cold) did you have?

Where did the action in the dream take place?

When was it set? Did you see lots of characters from your past, or did you even feel it was set in the future?

Why do you think you had this dream now? Did it link to something you're worrying about, or looking forward to, at the moment? Does it have elements of something you've just done?

Handy Hints

It's easy to let a dream fade away before you can capture the details. To prevent this from happening all the time, try these things:

If you're in a rush, write really quick notes. Try to find time later to look back on your notes and see if you remember any more detail.

Write down EVERYTHING. Even tiny details might be important. Think about numbers, colours, the weather, clothes...you might remember this sort of detail even if you can't remember the main theme of the dream.

Draw pictures if it's quicker or easier than writing everything down in words. Don't be shy – no-one else will see how good or bad your drawings are!

Don't even get out of bed before you write in your Dream Diary. Try to stay as close to your sleepy state as you can.

Now you're in the best position to analyse your own dreams.

Date: _____ ⏰ **Time:** _____

Before I slept I was thinking about: _____

My dream: I was on an aeroplane with mum. She was telling me about a plane crash when our plane started to fall. I put my seat belt on and my mask then started to rumage in my bag I got out our hamster Ben. I held him up to a mask, when started to walk up the tube. I stopped him by squaring it. The plane

~~I think it means:~~ had leveled out so I put Ben in his ball. Mum was doing something so I checked on Ben. His ball was empty I crawled down the isle and found Ben 4 seats down. I carried him back up to my seat and asked mum what I should do with him. She

~~Date:~~ didn't answer so I asked ⏰ ~~Time:~~ a flight attendant.

~~Before I slept I was thinking about:~~ I was given a little pack containing small rolls of twigs. The pilot gave an anouncement telling me the twigs were a raft to send Ben home on. I was

My dream: out cold and told mum Ben would jump off and drown. Scene changed. Still on plane but with 4 seats facing strangers Badger, my cat, was lying on the table and I was still playing with Ben. I put him in his ball among our bags so he couldn't escape. I look in my bag and moan 'oh no' Mum 'Whats wrong' Me: 'I think

I think it means: I left my MP3 at home. Mum 'Where you listening to it last night?' Me 'I think so. Mum "you'll have left it on your bedside table. I was wondering is she was psycic coz I left it exactly there.

Date: 15/06/06   ⏰ **Time:**

Before I slept I was thinking about: My work experience

My dream: I was just leaving school when I saw a quad with 5 people on and Stuart Ward driving. I wished I could have a go but there was no space. Just down the road Stuart dropped them off, so I asked for a backy. I tried standing on the back but I slipped, so Stuart made me sit

I think it means: On the seat. He dropped me off at Chatsworth square next to our car. I got in and turned to offer him a ride, but he was gone. We followed him.

I woke up before the end of the dream

Recurring themes in my dreams

☆ 1 I don't notice others except possibly pets.

☆

2. Because I was walking on a

☆ road, It seems to be my life path, and because there

☆ were people it means I am afraid of walking it alone.

☆

Some might say...

"When our memories outweigh our dreams, we have grown old."

Bill Clinton

Date:_____ ⏰ **Time;**_____
Before I slept I was thinking about:_____
_____

My dream: I was shopping with sophie and becky. We went though a door + up some *spiral* twisty stairs into a large room. It was hot + suffocating so I left. We went into a hall where S + B sat down. I stood and watched people dancing. I watched 2 men. One wearing a yellow sequin dress, the other a green sequin dress. They wore odd shoes, one silver one green

I think it means: like they had swapped a shoe. The does her sequins as well.
_____
_____

Date:_____ ⏰ **Time;**_____
Before I slept I was thinking about:_____
_____

My dream:_____
_____
_____
_____
_____

I think it means:_____
_____
_____
_____

Date: _____ ⏰ Time: _____

Before I slept I was thinking about: _____

_____

_____

My dream: _____

_____

_____

_____

_____

I think it means: _____

_____

_____

_____

Recurring themes in my dreams

☆ _____

_____

☆ _____

_____

☆ _____

_____

☆ _____

_____

☆ _____

_____

Did you know...

People who have become blind still see images and scenes in their dreams. If they were born blind, though, they dream about sounds, smells and things they can touch.

Date:_____ ⏰ Time;_____
Before I slept I was thinking about:_____
_____
_____

My dream:_____
_____
_____
_____
_____
_____

I think it means:_____
_____
_____
_____

Date:_____ ⏰ Time;_____
Before I slept I was thinking about:_____
_____
_____

My dream:_____
_____
_____
_____
_____

I think it means:_____
_____
_____
_____

Date:_____ 🕐 Time:_____

Before I slept I was thinking about:_____

_____

_____

My dream:_____

_____

_____

_____

_____

I think it means:_____

_____

_____

_____

Recurring themes in my dreams

☆_____

_____

☆_____

_____

☆_____

_____

☆_____

_____

☆_____

_____

Some might say...

'A Dream Within a Dream'

All that we see or seem
Is but a dream within a dream.

Edgar Allan Poe

Date:_____ ⏰ Time;_____

Before I slept I was thinking about:_____

_____

_____

My dream:_____

_____

_____

_____

_____

I think it means:_____

_____

_____

_____

Date:_____ ⏰ Time;_____

Before I slept I was thinking about:_____

_____

_____

My dream:_____

_____

_____

_____

_____

I think it means:_____

_____

_____

_____

Date:_____ ⏰ Time;_____

Before I slept I was thinking about:_____

_____

_____

My dream:_____

_____

_____

_____

_____

I think it means:_____

_____

_____

_____

Recurring themes in my dreams

☆_____

_____

☆_____

_____

☆_____

_____

☆_____

_____

☆_____

_____

Did you know...

Salvador Dali – the famous surrealist artist – believed that he could paint a dream directly from his unconscious mind, without his conscious mind ever getting in the way!

And... relax

MOVING MEDITATION

Before you sleep, go for a walk! Just around your bedroom – but concentrate your whole mind on every step. Think about how your legs are moving, and how your feet touch the floor. You should start to feel more graceful and relaxed.

ARTY SMARTY

Every night, take time to really study a painting. It could be a famous one from a book, or any other with lots of detail. Sink into the picture and think about everything that you see in it. Allow your mind to drift to wherever the painting takes it!

SILENT SPEAKING

Lean back, close your eyes, and choose a word to say to yourself. Breathe in and out, saying the word in your head every time you exhale. Try this for up to 20 minutes to clear your thoughts.

TIME FOR BED

Lie on your bed and close your eyes. Concentrate on each part of your body, bit by bit. Think about your toes, then your feet, then your ankles, and work all the way up to your head. Tense and relax each set of muscles as you think about them.

DEEP THOUGHT

Close your eyes and imagine looking down inside yourself, to the very centre of calm within you. Whatever happens in the world outside, you have a safe place deep inside you.

DEEP BREATHING

Sit nice and straight and imagine your body is a tall building. Breathe in, as if you're trying to fill the first floor with air. Breathe out, and feel the change in your chest. Breathe deeper next time, to fill the second floor with air. With every breath in, try to fill another level of the building.

FACING FACTS

Watch your reflection as you lift your shoulders up to your ears. Count to five then drop them and gently move your head from side to side. Now scrunch your face up tightly for five, and relax. Finally, open your mouth in the widest yawn you can, and stick out your tongue. Hold for five and release.

WAR ON WAKEFULNESS

Stand with your hands by your side and feet about a metre apart, toes forward. Turn your left foot so your toes point out to the side. Gently bend your left knee so you're nearer the floor. Raise your arms above your head, then slowly lower them until your left one is over your bent leg, and your right one straight behind you. Take five deep breaths, then stand straight again. Do the same on your right side.

Date: _____ ⏰ Time; _____
Before I slept I was thinking about: _____
_____
_____

My dream: _____
_____
_____
_____
_____

I think it means: _____
_____
_____
_____

Date: _____ ⏰ Time; _____
Before I slept I was thinking about: _____
_____
_____

My dream: _____
_____
_____
_____
_____

I think it means: _____
_____
_____
_____

Date: _____ ⏰ Time: _____

Before I slept I was thinking about:

_____

My dream:

_____

_____

_____

_____

I think it means:

_____

_____

_____

Recurring themes in my dreams

☆ _____

_____

☆ _____

_____

☆ _____

_____

☆ _____

_____

☆ _____

_____

Some might say...

'The Dream'

Dear love, for nothing less than thee
Would I have broke this happy dream,

John Donne

Date:_____ ⏰ Time;_____

Before I slept I was thinking about:_____

_____

_____

My dream:_____

_____

_____

_____

_____

I think it means:_____

_____

_____

_____

_____

Date:_____ ⏰ Time;_____

Before I slept I was thinking about:_____

_____

_____

My dream:_____

_____

_____

_____

_____

I think it means:_____

_____

_____

_____

_____

Date:_____ ⏰ Time:_____

Before I slept I was thinking about:_____

_____

_____

My dream:_____

_____

_____

_____

_____

I think it means:_____

_____

_____

_____

Recurring themes in my dreams

☆_____

_____

☆_____

_____

☆_____

_____

☆_____

_____

☆_____

_____

Did you know...

Our body temperature and brain's sleep cycles are closely linked. If we are too hot or too cold our sleep can become lighter and our REM sleep can be interrupted.

Date:_____ ⏰ Time;_____

Before I slept I was thinking about:_____
_____

My dream:_____
_____
_____
_____
_____

I think it means:_____
_____
_____
_____

Date:_____ ⏰ Time;_____

Before I slept I was thinking about:_____
_____

My dream:_____
_____
_____
_____
_____

I think it means:_____
_____
_____
_____

Date: _____ ⏰ Time: _____

Before I slept I was thinking about: _____

_____

_____

My dream: _____

_____

_____

_____

_____

I think it means: _____

_____

_____

_____

Recurring themes in my dreams

☆ _____

_____

☆ _____

_____

☆ _____

_____

☆ _____

_____

☆ _____

_____

Some might say...

'The Higher Pantheism'

Dreams are true while they last, and do we not live in dreams?

Tennyson

Date: _____ ⏰ Time: _____
Before I slept I was thinking about: _____
_____

My dream: _____
_____
_____
_____
_____

I think it means: _____
_____
_____
_____

Date: _____ ⏰ Time: _____
Before I slept I was thinking about: _____
_____

My dream: _____
_____
_____
_____
_____

I think it means: _____
_____
_____
_____

Date:_____ ⏰Time:_____

Before I slept I was thinking about:_____

_____

_____

My dream:_____

_____

_____

_____

_____

I think it means:_____

_____

_____

_____

Recurring themes in my dreams

☆_____

_____

☆_____

_____

☆_____

_____

☆_____

_____

☆_____

_____

Did you know...

Scientific studies show that your brain is actually more active when you're asleep than when you're awake.

Sleep patterns

An important part of dreaming is the times that you do it.
Scientists have discovered different types of sleep which form a cycle. After you've dropped off, you fall into a deep sleep. Your brain activity slows down and your muscles become totally relaxed.

Most of your body's basic activities, such as heartbeat and breathing, slow down as you sleep, but your brain stays active all night, receiving sense signals.

While you dream

After about an hour of this deep sleep, your brain starts to speed up. Your eyes flicker behind your closed eyelids and most of your dreams happen during this stage. It's called REM sleep, which stands for Rapid Eye Movement – because of the way your eyes are moving. Strangely enough, your body is unable to move during this sleep – this may be a way of keeping you safe while you dream.

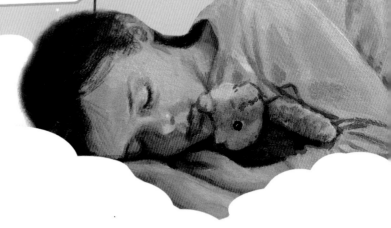

'Reading' signals

Billions of nerve signals flash around the brain every second, bringing information from the senses, sending out instructions to the muscles, and carrying thoughts and memories.

REM

Your brain goes through the cycle of deep to REM sleep about every hour and a half. Scientists believe that you're most likely to remember your dreams if you wake up during REM sleep. It's best if you can wake up naturally in the morning as you move out of this stage.

Date: _____ ⏰ Time; _____
Before I slept I was thinking about: _____

_____

My dream: _____

_____

_____

_____

I think it means: _____

_____

_____

Date: _____ ⏰ Time; _____
Before I slept I was thinking about: _____

_____

My dream: _____

_____

_____

_____

I think it means: _____

_____

_____

_____

Date: Time:

Before I slept I was thinking about:

My dream:

I think it means:

Recurring themes in my dreams

☆ _____

☆ _____

☆ _____

☆ _____

☆ _____

Some might say...

"If a little dreaming is dangerous, the cure for it is not to dream less but to dream more, to dream all the time."

Marcel Proust

Date:_____ ⏰Time;_____
Before I slept I was thinking about:_____
_____
_____
My dream:_____
_____
_____
_____
_____
I think it means:_____
_____
_____
_____
_____

Date:_____ ⏰Time;_____
Before I slept I was thinking about:_____
_____
_____
My dream:_____
_____
_____
_____
_____
I think it means:_____
_____
_____
_____

Date:_____ ⏰ Time:_____

Before I slept I was thinking about:_____

_____

_____

My dream:_____

_____

_____

_____

_____

I think it means:_____

_____

_____

_____

Recurring themes in my dreams

☆_____

_____

☆_____

_____

☆_____

_____

☆_____

_____

☆_____

_____

Did you know...

Most people in men's dreams are other men. Women dream equally about men and women.

Date:_____ ⏰ Time;_____
Before I slept I was thinking about:_____
_____
_____

My dream:_____
_____
_____
_____
_____

I think it means:_____
_____
_____
_____

Date:_____ ⏰ Time;_____
Before I slept I was thinking about:_____
_____
_____

My dream:_____
_____
_____
_____
_____

I think it means:_____
_____
_____
_____

Date:_____ ⏰Time:_____

Before I slept I was thinking about:_____

_____

_____

My dream:_____

_____

_____

_____

_____

I think it means:_____

_____

_____

_____

Recurring themes in my dreams

☆ _____

_____

☆ _____

_____

☆ _____

_____

☆ _____

_____

☆ _____

_____

Some might say...

"For life is but a dream
whose shapes return,
Some frequently, some
seldom, some by night
And some by day."

James Thompson

Date:_____ Time;_____
Before I slept I was thinking about:_____
_____
_____
My dream:_____
_____
_____
_____
_____
I think it means:_____
_____
_____
_____
_____

Date:_____ Time;_____
Before I slept I was thinking about:_____
_____
_____
My dream:_____
_____
_____
_____
_____
I think it means:_____
_____
_____
_____
_____

Date: _____ ⏰ Time: _____

Before I slept I was thinking about: _____

_____

_____

My dream: _____

_____

_____

_____

_____

I think it means: _____

_____

_____

_____

Recurring themes in my dreams

☆ _____

_____

☆ _____

_____

☆ _____

_____

☆ _____

_____

☆ _____

_____

Did you know...

You spend a third of your life sleeping. That means you can have been in a dream world for a total of six years!

Dream quiz

1 How long does it take you to fall asleep at night?

a. Ages – up to an hour. ☐
b. About 2-5 minutes. ☐
c. Between 10 and 20 minutes. ☑

2 Do you normally appear in your own dreams?

a. No, I always dream about other people. ☐
b. I can't really remember my dreams. ☐
c. Sometimes, often as the main person. ☑

3 What's your favourite night-time drink?

a. Coke or fruit juice. ☐
b. A cup of tea or coffee. ☐
c. Milk or hot chocolate. ☑

4 How often do you have nightmares?

a. Really regularly, and they're well scary. ☐
b. Never – at least, not that I remember. ☐
c. Every now and then. ☑

5 What do you do before you go to sleep at night?

a. Play on my computer. ☐
b. Watch TV in bed. ☐
c. Read a book. ☑

6 What time do you go to bed?

a. It depends – sometimes 8 pm, sometimes 11 pm. ☑
b. As late as possible – midnight at the weekends. ☐
c. Usually around 9 or 9.30. ☐

7

What time do you get up?

a. As late as possible. ☐

b. About 7 am unless it's a weekend, then it's more like midday! ☐

c. About 7 am for school, sometimes I'll lie in until 8 am if I can. ☑

8

What's your favourite way to sleep?

a. I toss and turn all night so lots of ways. ☐

b. Anyway – flat on my back, curled up, on my stomach. ☐

c. Curled up on my side, cosy and warm. ☑

How did you score?

Mostly As

Eek! You're not going the right way to get a good night's sleep. Your sleep patterns are all out of sync and it's disrupting your dreams. Try to make your bedtime and getting up time regular, and don't play computer games before bed! Read all the 'c' answers for an idea of a better sleep routine.

Mostly Bs

Yikes! You're not exactly Sleeping Beauty, either! It sounds like you're overtired, even though you're sleeping a lot. You may sleep so deeply that you don't remember your dreams like many people do. Again, read the 'c' answers to see what will bring a better bedtime.

⚞Mostly Cs

Well done you! You're doing all the right things for a dream-filled sleep that will also leave you feeling refreshed every morning. Now all you need to do is keep up-to-date with your dream diary!

Date: _____ ⏰ Time; _____
Before I slept I was thinking about: _____
_____

My dream: _____
_____
_____
_____
_____

I think it means: _____
_____
_____
_____
_____

Date: _____ ⏰ Time; _____
Before I slept I was thinking about: _____
_____

My dream: _____
_____
_____
_____
_____

I think it means: _____
_____
_____
_____
_____

Date: _____ ⏰ Time: _____

Before I slept I was thinking about:

_____

_____

My dream:

_____

_____

_____

_____

I think it means:

_____

_____

_____

_____

Recurring themes in my dreams

☆ _____

_____

☆ _____

_____

☆ _____

_____

☆ _____

_____

☆ _____

_____

Some might say...

'He Wishes For
The Cloths of Heaven'

I have spread my dreams
under your feet;
Tread softly because you
tread on my dreams.

W. B. Yeats

Date:_____ ⏰ Time;_____
Before I slept I was thinking about:_____
_____
_____

My dream:_____
_____
_____
_____
_____
_____

I think it means:_____
_____
_____
_____
_____

Date:_____ ⏰ Time;_____
Before I slept I was thinking about:_____
_____
_____

My dream:_____
_____
_____
_____
_____
_____

I think it means:_____
_____
_____
_____
_____

Date:_____ ⏰ Time:_____

Before I slept I was thinking about:_____

_____

My dream:_____

_____

_____

_____

I think it means:_____

_____

_____

_____

Recurring themes in my dreams

☆_____

_____

☆_____

_____

☆_____

_____

☆_____

_____

☆_____

_____

Did you know...

The word 'dream' may come from an old word meaning 'song', although it seems likely that the word 'swefn' meaning sleep was used hundreds of years ago.

Date:_____ ⏰ Time:_____

Before I slept I was thinking about:_____

_____

_____

My dream:_____

_____

_____

_____

_____

I think it means:_____

_____

_____

_____

Date:_____ ⏰ Time:_____

Before I slept I was thinking about:_____

_____

_____

My dream:_____

_____

_____

_____

_____

I think it means:_____

_____

_____

_____

Date:_____ ⏰ Time:_____

Before I slept I was thinking about:_____

_____

_____

My dream:_____

_____

_____

_____

_____

I think it means:_____

_____

_____

_____

Recurring themes in my dreams

☆_____
_____
☆_____
_____
☆_____
_____
☆_____
_____
☆_____
_____

Some might say...

From
Hamlet

To sleep: perchance to dream:
ay, there's the rub.

Shakespeare

Pillow Talk

Scientists have proved that everyone dreams – even tiny babies do it. Not everyone remembers their dreams – some people feel they haven't even had any. You can train yourself to remember lots about your dreams, though. As well as learning to write in your Dream Diary (see page 54) you can prepare yourself before you fall asleep...

1 Set your alarm a little earlier than normal. If you wake during your dream-sleep you're more likely to remember the details clearly.

2 Read your Dream Diary. It's a great way to help remember new dreams.

3 Write down what's happened to you during the day. Then you'll be able to look back and see if there's any link between actual events and your dreams.

4 When you turn out the light, say a little dream ditty over and over to yourself. How about: "Dreams, dreams, come to me, make things as clear as they can be."

Top Score

Not everyone feels the same about their dreams. Some people like to feature as the main character, others prefer to dream nice things about their loved ones. Here's one way to categorize your dreams, but you can change the scores and their order if you wish.

1 Horrid! A nightmare involving the people you love the most.

2 Scary! A nightmare involving yourself.

3 Yuck! A nightmare about people you don't really know.

4 Help! A dream where you can't change what's happening to you.

5 Hmm! A dream where things are happening but you're just watching.

6 See saw! A whole muddle of good things and not so nice things.

7 Crazy! A dream that leaves you reeling because it zooms all over the place.

8 Yay! A positive dream about good things happening to you.

9 Excellent! A lovely dream about good things happening to people you love.

10 Right on! A great dream where you make good things happen.

Date: _____ 🕐 Time: _____
Before I slept I was thinking about: _____
_____

My dream: _____
_____
_____
_____

I think it means: _____
_____
_____
_____

Date: _____ 🕐 Time: _____
Before I slept I was thinking about: _____
_____

My dream: _____
_____
_____
_____

I think it means: _____
_____
_____
_____

Date: Time;

Before I slept I was thinking about:

My dream:

I think it means:

Recurring themes in my dreams

☆ _____

☆ _____

☆ _____

☆ _____

☆ _____

Some might say...

From
*A Midsummer
Night's Dream*
The eye of man hath not
heard, the ear of man hath not
seen, man's hand is not able to
taste, his tongue to conceive,
nor his heart to report, what
my dream was.
Shakespeare

Date:_____ ⏰ Time;_____
Before I slept I was thinking about:_____
_____
_____

My dream:_____
_____
_____
_____
_____

I think it means:_____
_____
_____
_____

Date:_____ ⏰ Time;_____
Before I slept I was thinking about:_____
_____
_____

My dream:_____
_____
_____
_____
_____

I think it means:_____
_____
_____
_____

Date:_____ ⏰ Time:_____

Before I slept I was thinking about:_____

_____

_____

My dream:_____

_____

_____

_____

_____

I think it means:_____

_____

_____

_____

_____

Recurring themes in my dreams

☆_____

_____

☆_____

_____

☆_____

_____

☆_____

_____

☆_____

_____

Did you know...

Teenagers need just as much sleep as small children – about 10 hours. For the average adult aged 25–55, eight hours is considered ideal. Those aged 65 and over need the least sleep of all – about six hours.

Date:_____ ⏰ Time;_____

Before I slept I was thinking about:_____

_____

_____

My dream:_____

_____

_____

_____

_____

I think it means:_____

_____

_____

_____

Date:_____ ⏰ Time;_____

Before I slept I was thinking about:_____

_____

_____

My dream:_____

_____

_____

_____

_____

I think it means:_____

_____

_____

_____

Date: _____ ⏰ Time: _____

Before I slept I was thinking about: _____
_____
_____

My dream: _____
_____
_____
_____
_____

I think it means: _____
_____
_____
_____

Recurring themes in my dreams

☆ _____
_____
☆ _____
_____
☆ _____
_____
☆ _____
_____
☆ _____
_____

Some might say...

'To Night'
Swiftly walk o'er the
western wave,
Spirit of Night!
Out of the misty eastern cave,
Where, all the long and
lone daylight,
Thou wovest dreams
of joy and fear.

Shelley

Date:_____ ⏰Time:_____
Before I slept I was thinking about:_____
_____
_____

My dream:_____
_____
_____
_____
_____

I think it means:_____
_____
_____
_____

Date:_____ ⏰Time:_____
Before I slept I was thinking about:_____
_____
_____

My dream:_____
_____
_____
_____
_____

I think it means:_____
_____
_____
_____

Date:_____ ⏰ Time:_____

Before I slept I was thinking about:_____

_____

My dream:_____

_____

_____

_____

_____

I think it means:_____

_____

_____

_____

Recurring themes in my dreams

☆_____

_____

☆_____

_____

☆_____

_____

☆_____

_____

☆_____

_____

Did you know...

The ancient Romans kept a record of their dreams. They sometimes told their leaders about very vivid dreams in case they were important to the town or empire.

Date: _____ 🕐 Time: _____
Before I slept I was thinking about: _____

My dream: _____

I think it means: _____

Date: _____ 🕐 Time: _____
Before I slept I was thinking about: _____

My dream: _____

I think it means: _____

Date: _____ ⏰ Time: _____

Before I slept I was thinking about:

_____

My dream:

_____
_____
_____

I think it means:

_____
_____
_____

Recurring themes in my dreams

☆ _____
☆ _____
☆ _____
☆ _____
☆ _____

Some might say...

Traditional

Row, row, row your boat
Gently down the stream.
Merrily, merrily,
merrily, merrily,
Life is but a dream!

Have you ever wondered about what happenend next in a dream that you never finished? Perhaps you were about to travel the world, become the Prime Minister or a famous pop star! Use these pages to finish off those dreams, however you decide. Use your dreams as a springboard for a fantastic story and let your imagination run riot...

Inspiration

Who do you most admire?
Imagine a day in their life, and
write about all the fun you
would have!

Inspiration

Where is your dream holiday destination? Write about what the weather would be like, and who you would meet there.

Inspiration

Where would you go if you were invisible and what would you do?

Inspiration

Write about your scariest nightmare. How did it start and how would you like it to end?

Date: _____ 🕐 Time: _____
Where I was: _____
What I daydreamt: _____
_____
_____
Who was in it: _____
I think it means: _____
_____
_____

Date: _____ 🕐 Time: _____
Where I was: _____
What I daydreamt: _____
_____
_____
Who was in it: _____
I think it means: _____
_____
_____

Date: _____ 🕐 Time: _____
Where I was: _____
What I daydreamt: _____
_____
_____
Who was in it: _____
I think it means: _____
_____
_____

Date: _____ 🕐 Time: _____
Where I was: _____
What I daydreamt: _____
_____
_____
Who was in it: _____
I think it means: _____
_____
_____

Date: _____ 🕐 Time: _____
Where I was: _____
What I daydreamt: _____
_____
_____
Who was in it: _____
I think it means: _____
_____
_____

Recurring themes in my daydreams

* _____
* _____
* _____
* _____
* _____

Some might say...

"Dream no small dreams for they have no power to move the hearts of men."

Goethe

Date:_____ ⏰Time:_____
Where I was:_____
What I daydreamt: _____
_____
_____

Who was in it:_____
I think it means:_____
_____
_____

Date:_____ ⏰Time:_____
Where I was:_____
What I daydreamt: _____
_____
_____

Who was in it:_____
I think it means:_____
_____
_____

Date:_____ ⏰Time:_____
Where I was:_____
What I daydreamt: _____
_____
_____

Who was in it:_____
I think it means:_____
_____
_____

Date:_____ 🕐 Time:_____
Where I was:_____
What I daydreamt: _____
_____
_____

Who was in it:_____
I think it means:_____
_____
_____

Date:_____ 🕐 Time:_____
Where I was:_____
What I daydreamt: _____
_____
_____

Who was in it:_____
I think it means:_____
_____
_____

Recurring themes in my daydreams

✳ _____
✳ _____
✳ _____
✳ _____
✳ _____

Did you know...

Many years ago, people thought that dreams were caused by indigestion!

Date: _____ ⏰ Time: _____
Where I was: _____
What I daydreamt: _____
_____
_____
_____
Who was in it: _____
I think it means: _____
_____
_____

Date: _____ ⏰ Time: _____
Where I was: _____
What I daydreamt: _____
_____
_____
_____
Who was in it: _____
I think it means: _____
_____
_____

Date: _____ ⏰ Time: _____
Where I was: _____
What I daydreamt: _____
_____
_____
_____
Who was in it: _____
I think it means: _____
_____
_____

Date:_____ 🕐 Time:_____

Where I was:_____

What I daydreamt:_____

_____

_____

Who was in it:_____

I think it means:_____

_____

_____

Date:_____ 🕐 Time:_____

Where I was:_____

What I daydreamt:_____

_____

_____

Who was in it:_____

I think it means:_____

_____

_____

Recurring themes in my daydreams

* ❄ _____
* ❄ _____
* ❄ _____
* ❄ _____
* ❄ _____

Some might say...

"Your vision will become clear only when you look into your heart. Who looks outside, dreams. Who looks inside, awakens."

Carl Jung

Date:_____ ⏰ Time:_____
Where I was:_____
What I daydreamt: _____
_____
_____
_____

Who was in it:_____
I think it means:_____
_____
_____

Date:_____ ⏰ Time:_____
Where I was:_____
What I daydreamt: _____
_____
_____
_____

Who was in it:_____
I think it means:_____
_____
_____

Date:_____ ⏰ Time:_____
Where I was:_____
What I daydreamt: _____
_____
_____
_____

Who was in it:_____
I think it means:_____
_____
_____

Date: _____ ⏰ Time: _____
Where I was: _____
What I daydreamt: _____
_____
_____

Who was in it: _____
I think it means: _____
_____
_____

Date: _____ ⏰ Time: _____
Where I was: _____
What I daydreamt: _____
_____
_____

Who was in it: _____
I think it means: _____
_____
_____

Recurring themes in my daydreams

* _____
* _____
* _____
* _____
* _____

Did you know...

The ancient Egyptians kept records of dreams, and had their own 'dream dictionaries' full of meanings and interpretations.

Date:_____ 🕐 Time:_____

Where I was:_____

What I daydreamt: _____

_____

Who was in it:_____

I think it means:_____

_____

_____

Date:_____ 🕐 Time:_____

Where I was:_____

What I daydreamt: _____

_____

Who was in it:_____

I think it means:_____

_____

_____

Date:_____ 🕐 Time:_____

Where I was:_____

What I daydreamt: _____

_____

Who was in it:_____

I think it means:_____

_____

_____

Date: _____ 🕐 Time: _____

Where I was: _____

What I daydreamt: _____

_____

_____

Who was in it: _____

I think it means: _____

_____

_____

Date: _____ 🕐 Time: _____

Where I was: _____

What I daydreamt: _____

_____

_____

Who was in it: _____

I think it means: _____

_____

_____

Recurring themes in my daydreams

* * _____
* * _____
* * _____
* * _____
* * _____

Some might say...

From
The Tempest

We are such stuff
As dreams are made on,
and our little life
Is rounded with a sleep.

Shakespeare

Date: _____ 🕑 Time: _____
Where I was: _____
What I daydreamt: _____
_____
_____

Who was in it: _____
I think it means: _____
_____
_____

Date: _____ 🕑 Time: _____
Where I was: _____
What I daydreamt: _____
_____
_____

Who was in it: _____
I think it means: _____
_____
_____

Date: _____ 🕑 Time: _____
Where I was: _____
What I daydreamt: _____
_____
_____

Who was in it: _____
I think it means: _____
_____
_____

Date:_____ ⏰ Time:_____
Where I was:_____
What I daydreamt: _____
_____
_____
Who was in it:_____
I think it means:_____
_____
_____

Date:_____ ⏰ Time:_____
Where I was:_____
What I daydreamt: _____
_____
_____
Who was in it:_____
I think it means:_____
_____
_____

Recurring themes in my daydreams

✳ _____
✳ _____
✳ _____
✳ _____
✳ _____

Did you know...

Catnaps can improve alertness. The ideal catnap should last about 90 minutes, so that you have enough time to run through one full sleep cycle.

Date: _____ 🕐 Time: _____

Where I was: _____

What I daydreamt: _____

_____

_____

_____

Who was in it: _____

I think it means: _____

_____

_____

Date: _____ 🕐 Time: _____

Where I was: _____

What I daydreamt: _____

_____

_____

_____

Who was in it: _____

I think it means: _____

_____

_____

Date: _____ 🕐 Time: _____

Where I was: _____

What I daydreamt: _____

_____

_____

_____

Who was in it: _____

I think it means: _____

_____

_____

Date: _____ 🕐 Time: _____
Where I was: _____
What I daydreamt: _____
_____
_____

Who was in it: _____
I think it means: _____
_____
_____

Date: _____ 🕐 Time: _____
Where I was: _____
What I daydreamt: _____
_____
_____

Who was in it: _____
I think it means: _____
_____

Recurring themes in my daydreams

* _____
* _____
* _____
* _____
* _____

Some might say...

Hyperion
As when, upon a tranced summer-night,
Dream, and so dream all night without a stir.
Keats

Date: _____ 🕐 Time: _____
Where I was: _____
What I daydreamt: _____
_____
_____
Who was in it: _____
I think it means: _____
_____
_____

Date: _____ 🕐 Time: _____
Where I was: _____
What I daydreamt: _____
_____
_____
Who was in it: _____
I think it means: _____
_____
_____

Date: _____ 🕐 Time: _____
Where I was: _____
What I daydreamt: _____
_____
_____
Who was in it: _____
I think it means: _____
_____
_____

Date:_____ ⏰ Time:_____

Where I was:_____

What I daydreamt: _____

_____

_____

Who was in it:_____

I think it means:_____

_____

_____

Date:_____ ⏰ Time:_____

Where I was:_____

What I daydreamt: _____

_____

_____

Who was in it:_____

I think it means:_____

_____

_____

Recurring themes in my daydreams

✳ _____

✳ _____

✳ _____

✳ _____

✳ _____

Did you know...

Everyone dreams,
even babies and toddlers.
Some scientists even think
that animals dream too.

First published in 2005 by
Miles Kelly Publishing Ltd
Bardfield Centre, Great Bardfield, Essex, CM7 4SL

Copyright © Miles Kelly Publishing Ltd 2005

2 4 6 8 10 9 7 5 3 1

Editorial Director
Belinda Gallagher

Senior Editor
Jenni Rainford

Assistant Editor
Hannah Todd

Designers
Louisa Leitao, Helen Weller

Production
Estela Boulton

Picture Research Manager
Liberty Newton

Picture Researcher
Laura Faulder

Scanning and Reprographics
Anthony Cambray, Mike Coupe, Ian Paulyn

ISBN 1-84236-562-2

Printed in Thailand

British Library Cataloguing-in-Publication Data
A catalogue record for this book is available from the British Library

All artworks are from Miles Kelly Artwork Bank

All pictures from the Miles Kelly Archives:
Castrol, CMCD, Corbis, Corel, DigitalSTOCK, digitalvision, Flat Earth,
Hemera, ILN, John Foxx, PhotoAlto, PhotoDisc,
PhotoEssentials, PhotoPro, Stockbyte

www.mileskelly.net
info@mileskelly.net